But Is It In The Bible?

Doctrines and Practices Measured by
The New Testament Alone

DAVID P. NOLTE

Charleston, SC
www.PalmettoPublishing.com

But Is It In The Bible?
Copyright © 2021 by David P. Nolte

All rights reserved

No portion of this book may be reproduced, stored in a retrieval system, or transmitted in any form by any means—electronic, mechanical, photocopy, recording, or other—except for brief quotations in printed reviews, without prior permission of the author.

Paperback ISBN: 978-1-68515-640-4
eBook ISBN: 978-1-68515-641-1

PREFACE:
A Letter to the readers

At the outset, let me assure the reader that I believe that we are saved by grace through faith. We do not earn, merit, or work for salvation. It is a free gift, paid for and delivered by Jesus. But it is appropriated by faith.

Faith is always more than mere "head stuff." It is more than mere assent to the truth of a proposition. Faith always includes belief, trust, and obedience. This can be clearly seen in Abraham, who believed God (and showed it by trusting God and in doing what God told him to do). Separate out trust and obedience and faith becomes a diminished takeoff of the real thing.

For the believers in Jesus, there is one litmus for truth. It is not the opinion of man, not the teachings of any human, however persuasive, and is not the conclusion of any church council or denomination. It is the clear "Thus says the Lord," as recorded in the New Testament.

What agrees with the New Testament is of God. What contradicts, adds to, alters, or takes away from the New Testament is Satanic.

Where, and what, the Scripture speaks, we speak. Where the Scripture does not speak is an area of free opinion: "Do we worship at 10:00 or 11:00?", "Do we sing traditional hymns or may we use more contemporary, but Biblically correct, songs?" or, "Is the King James Version the version of the Bible God dropped from Heaven on a Golden Chain, or is a more modern version acceptable?"

To the end that we do not copy the Pharisees, we declare: "In essentials, unity; in opinions, liberty; and in all things, love." What is essential is who Jesus is, His relationship to God, what He did, and what He commanded in the Gospels, and what He taught us through the inspired writings of those who penned the New Testament scrolls.

The Christian Church and Churches of Christ express the focus of their teachings on Jesus Christ as Lord and humanity's only Savior – and that He is only Savior because He is Lord. He said, "He who has My commandments and keeps them is the one who loves Me; and he who loves Me will be loved by My Father, and I will love him and will disclose Myself to him." (John 14:21, NASB95).

Yours for sound, true, and faithful doctrine,
David P. Nolte.

Topics

PREFACE: A Letter to the readers · · · · · · · · · · · · · · · · · iii
THE THIEF ON THE CROSS · · · · · · · · · · · · · · · · · · · 1
BAPTISM · 4
ETERNAL SECURITY · 24
THE "SINNER'S PRAYER"
INVITING JESUS INTO YOUR HEART
"JUST RAISE YOUR HAND" · · · · · · · · · · · · · · · · · · · 38
THE RAPTURE · 40
GOD WON'T GIVE US MORE THAN WE
CAN HANDLE · 46
OTHER ISSUES · 53

THE THIEF ON THE CROSS
(Is not an excuse for not being baptized.)

One of the criminals who were hanged *there* was hurling abuse at Him, saying, "Are You not the Christ? Save Yourself and us." But the other answered, and rebuking him said, "Do you not even fear God, since you are under the same sentence of condemnation? And we indeed are *suffering justly*, for we are receiving what we deserve for our deeds; but this man has done nothing wrong." And he was saying, "Jesus, remember me when You come in Your kingdom!" And He said to him, "Truly I say to you, today you shall be with Me in Paradise." (Luke 23:39-43, NASB95).

Many people mistakenly look to the thief on the cross as an excuse for not being baptized.

"You need to repent and be baptized," we tell people, as Peter did on the Day of Pentecost. Those people, three thousand in number, did not say, "Oh, Peter! We don't need to be baptized because the thief on the cross wasn't."

But let us remember:

1. This event took place before Jesus died and, therefore, the Law was still in effect.

2. Christian baptism was not yet commanded, and was only first enjoined when Jesus ascended, saying,

> "All authority has been given to Me in heaven and on earth. Go therefore and make disciples of all the nations, baptizing them in the name of the Father and the Son and the Holy Spirit, teaching them to observe all that I commanded you; and lo, I am with you always, even to the end of the age." (Matt. 28:18-20, NASB95).Christian Baptism was first practiced on The

Day of Pentecost, fifty days later.

Therefore, the thief himself does not teach us anything about baptism, pro or con.

1. He couldn't have asked the Roman soldiers to let him take a "Baptism Break."

2. He didn't need to do what he had not yet been commanded to do by God. He didn't need to do what was an impossible thing for him to do.

Rather, look to Jesus who was Himself, though sinless, ready to be baptized to fulfill righteousness, to do the right thing.

BAPTISM

Recently, I attended a church camp and looked at the printed program for the week. On the back, it told the campers how to be saved. I was shocked and dismayed to find what I call "Gospel Lite!" (Not to be confused with Gospel Light, however!).

The plan was outlined like this:

1. Recognize that you are a sinner.

2. Decide to turn away from that sin.

3. Believe in Jesus Christ as God's Son.

4. Ask Him to come into your heart.

5. Pray the "Sinner's Prayer."

Now, while none of that is inherently wrong in itself, none of it can be definitively found in the New (or Old) Testament.

There are problems with it as it as practiced because:

1. It adds something that is not commanded in Scripture.

2. It stops short of what is commanded by God.

3. It takes on the form of a requirement for salvation.

It is like cooking a recipe with some of the ingredients missing, or with additional, but unnecessary, ingredients.

The real plan of salvation always includes baptism by immersion. It is never based on praying a certain prayer or inviting Jesus into your heart. Where, tell me *where*, is that commanded in the New Testament?

I asked the woman in charge of the church camp, "Where's baptism in this plan?"

She said, "Oh, I believe in baptism."

I said, "You'd never know it from what I read here."

She said, "Well, then, what would you tell them?"

I said, "I'd tell them what Peter told them on the day of Pentecost, 'Repent, and let each of you be baptized in the name of Jesus Christ for the forgiveness of your sins; and you shall receive the gift of the Holy Spirit.'"

The only book in the Bible where we see records of people becoming Christians after the Resurrection is the Book of Acts. The epistles were written to baptized believers to strengthen them, and to remind them of what being a baptized believer meant. Check out these New Covenant, conversions that follow and please observe what is common to every case of conversion in the Bible.

FIRST CONVERSION RECORD
The Multitude on the Day of Pentecost

> "Therefore let all the house of Israel know for certain that God has made Him both Lord and Christ—this Jesus whom you crucified." Now when they heard *this*, they were pierced to the heart, and said to Peter and the rest of the apostles, "Brethren, what shall we do?" Peter *said* to them, "Repent, and each of you be baptized in the name of Jesus Christ for the forgiveness of your sins; and you will receive the gift of the Holy Spiritt." (Acts 2:36-3, NASB95, italics in original).

Belief implied. Repentance evident. Baptism performed.

SECOND CONVERSION RECORD
The Samaritans

> But when they believed Philip preaching the good news about the kingdom of God and the name of Jesus Christ, they were being baptized, men and women alike. Even Simon himself believed; and after being baptized, he continued on with Philip, and as he observed signs and great miracles taking place, he was constantly amazed. (Acts 8:12-13, NASB95).

Belief stated. Repentance implied. Baptism performed.

THIRD CONVERSION RECORD
The Ethiopian Eunuch

> But an angel of the Lord spoke to Philip saying, "Get up and go south to the road that descends from Jerusalem to Gaza." (This is a desert *road*.) So he got up and went; and there was an Ethiopian eunuch, a court official of Candace, queen of the Ethiopians, who was in charge of all her treasure; and he had come to Jerusalem to worship, and he was returning and sitting in his chariot, and was reading the prophet Isaiah. Then the Spirit said to Philip, "Go up and join this chariot." Philip ran up and heard him

reading Isaiah the prophet, and said, "Do you understand what you are reading?" And he said, "Well, how could I, unless someone guides me?" And he invited Philip to come up and sit with him. Now the passage of Scripture which he was reading was this:

> "He was led as a sheep to slaughter;
> And as a lamb before its shearer is silent,
> So He does not open His mouth.
> In humiliation His judgment was taken away;
> Who will relate His generation?
> For His life is removed from the earth."

The eunuch answered Philip and said, "Please *tell* me, of whom does the prophet say this? Of himself or of someone else?" Then Philip opened his mouth, and beginning from this Scripture he preached Jesus to him. As they went along the road they came to some water; and the eunuch *said, "Look! Water! What prevents me from being baptized?" [And Philip said, "If you believe with all your heart, you may." And he answered and said, "I believe that Jesus Christ is the Son of God."] And he ordered the chariot to stop; and they both went down into the water, Philip as well

> as the eunuch, and he baptized him. (Acts 8:26-38, NASB95; italics in original).

Belief stated. Baptism performed.

FOURTH CONVERSION RECORD
Saul / Paul

Having been blinded by the Heavenly Vision of Jesus, Saul was led into Damascus and a man named Ananias was sent to him. So Ananias departed and entered the house, and after laying his hands on him said,

> "Brother Saul, the Lord Jesus, who appeared to you on the road by which you were coming, has sent me so that you may regain your sight and be filled with the Holy Spirit." And immediately there fell from his eyes something like scales, and he regained his sight, and he got up and was baptized; and he took food and was strengthened. Now for several days he was with the disciples who were at Damascus. (Acts 9:17-19, NASB95).

Belief implied. Repentance evident. Baptism performed.

FIFTH CONVERSION RECORD
Cornelius

When Peter was dispatched to the home of the Roman Centurion, and all who had gathered heard the Word of God, they received the Holy Spirit as God's approval of Gentile inclusion. Peter said,

> "Surely no one can refuse the water for these to be baptized who have received the Holy Spirit just as we *did*, can he?" (Acts 10:47, NASB95; italics in original).

Nothing about belief or repentance is mentioned here but baptism is performed.

SIXTH CONVERSION RECORD
Lydia

> A woman named Lydia, from the city of Thyatira, a seller of purple fabrics, a worshiper of God, was listening; and the Lord opened her heart to respond to the things spoken by Paul. And when she and her household had been baptized, she urged us, saying, "If you have judged me to be faithful to the Lord, come into my house and stay." And she prevailed upon us. (Acts 16:14-15, NASB95)

Belief Implied. Baptism performed.

SEVENTH CONVERSION RECORD
Jailer and household

After an earthquake opened the doors to all the cells in the jail where Paul and Silas were confined the jailer called for lights and rushed in, and

> ... trembling with fear he fell down before Paul and Silas, and after he brought them out, he said, "Sirs, what must I do to be saved?" They said, "Believe in the Lord Jesus, and you will be saved, you and your household." And they spoke the word of the Lord to him together with all who were in his house. And he took them that *very* hour of the night and washed their wounds, and immediately he was baptized, he and all his *household*. (Acts 16:29-33, NASB95; italics in original).

Belief implied. Repentance obvious. Baptism performed.

EIGHTH CONVERSION RECORD
Corinthians

When Silas and Timothy came down from Macedonia, to Corinth,

> ... Paul *began* devoting himself completely to the word, solemnly testifying to the Jews that Jesus was the Christ. But when they resisted and blasphemed, he shook out his garments and said to them, "Your blood *be* on your own heads! I am clean. From now on I will go to the Gentiles." Then he left there and went to the house of a man named Titius Justus, a worshiper of God, whose house was next to the synagogue. Crispus, the leader of the synagogue, believed in the Lord with all his household, and many of the Cor. when they heard were believing and being baptized. (Acts 18:5-8, NAS95; italics in original).

Belief stated. Repentance not mentioned. Baptism performed.

NINTH CONVERSION RECORD
Ephesians

> It happened that while Apollos was at Corinth, Paul passed through the upper country and came to Ephesus, and found some disciples. He said to them, "Did you receive the Holy Spirit when you believed?" And they *said* to him, "No, we have not even heard whether there is a Holy Spirit." And he said, "Into what then were you baptized?"

> And they said, "Into John's baptism." Paul said, "John baptized with the baptism of repentance, telling the people to believe in Him who was coming after him, that is, in Jesus." When they heard this, they were baptized in the name of the Lord Jesus." (Acts 19:1-5, NASB95; italics in original).

Wouldn't it appear that baptism was taught, commanded, and practiced on every occasion recorded in the Book of Acts when people became repentant believers?

Isn't it obvious that the early church put strong emphasis on baptism?

Then the epistles were written to those who had been baptized to correct problems, to encourage Christian growth, and so on. Don't look to the epistles for the plan of salvation. Except for those to whom they were written, the epistles wereare simple reminders of the terms of that plan.

Let's reason a little further:

Jesus Himself was baptized and said that it fulfilled righteousness in Matt. 3:15. Jesus then commanded that His disciples make other disciples, baptizing them and teaching them to observe all that He had commanded in: Matt. 28:18-20. One of His commandments is baptism and His. disciples are to obey that.

Baptism alone and apart from repentant belief, saves no one. That would be equivalent to diving into a swimming pool. There's nothing redemptive in that.

But baptism based on repentant belief, identifies us with, and corresponds to, what Christ did on the cross and in His resurrection.

Baptism without faith is empty, but faith without baptism is not complete.

Some might object to baptism being a work of merit.

But baptism is not a work at all since the one being baptized is passive. God does the work in baptism: forgiving sins and bestowing the gift of the Holy Spirit. (Acts 3:36-38). Baptism is immersion in water and God's bestowal of the Holy Spirit. It is being born of water and the Spirit. (John 3:1-3). Baptism does not add to or complete Christ's work, but it does identify us with the work and appropriates the benefit of the work He did in His death, burial, and resurrection. (Romans 6:1-4).

And if one gets caught up on this point, they should consider that belief is a work! People asked, "What shall we do, that we may work the works of God?" Jesus answered and said to them, "This is the work of God, that you believe in Him whom He has sent." (John 6:28-29, NASB95). The word for "work" here is "ergon" and means "that which one undertakes to do, enterprise, undertaking." This is Strong's Greek Number 2041.

Think a little further:

1. Jesus said that baptism fulfills righteousness.

That is, baptism is right. According to Jesus's own baptism in Matt. 3:13-15, it is, in fact, *righteous*.

If we know it is right to do and don't do it, it is a sin. James 4:17 makes that clear: "Remember, it is sin to know what you ought to do and then not do it." (Jas. 4:17, NLT).

2. Baptism is a command.

Jesus said to do it and the apostles commanded it.

How could anybody, who claims to have faith, hesitate to quickly obey whatever Jesus commanded? Baptism is not just an option;, it is a command. All we need to do is ask: "What did Jesus say?" and: "What am I going to do about it?"

So, if we know that something is a commandment and are still disobedient to it, there are several consequences:

What does it mean to claim to have faith, but yet to refuse to obey a clear command?

1. **We are no friend of Jesus**

    John 14:23 and John 15:14 teach us what Jesus requires of his friends. We are His friends if we obey Him.

2. **We cannot claim to truly know God:**

    1 John 2:3-6 says,

    "And how can we be sure that we belong to Him? By obeying His commandments. If someone says, "I belong to God," but doesn't obey God's commandments, that person is a liar and does not live in the truth. But those who obey God's word really do love Him. That is the way to know whether or not we live in Him. Those who say they live in God should live their lives as Christ did." (1 John 2:3-6, NLT).

3. **Nor can we claim to be saved without obedience:**

    Hebrews 5:8-9 says,

    "Even though Jesus was God's Son, He learned obedience from the things He suffered. In this way, God qualified Him as a perfect High Priest, and He became the source of eternal salvation for all those who obey Him." (Heb. 5:8-9, NLT).

4. Nor can we claim to possess the Holy Spirit without obedience:

"And we are witnesses of these things; and *so is* the Holy Spirit, whom God has given to those who obey Him." (Acts 5:32, NASB95).

Here are some Biblical associations with baptism:

1. New birth is associated with baptism:

In John 3:5, Jesus says,

"I assure you, no one can enter the Kingdom of God without being born of water and the Spirit." (John 3.5, NLT). Water here can only mean one of three things:

A. Human birth.
But importantly, the Bible never refers to human birth in reference to water. Besides, think of how unreasonable it would be to think that Jesus would say, "no one can enter the Kingdom of God without being born as a human and also being born of the Spirit." If one is not born as a human, he surely cannot be born of the Spirit!

B. The Holy Spirit.
The Bible never refers to the Holy Spirit as just "water." And think of the redundancy of, "no one can enter the Kingdom of God without being born of the Spirit also being born of the Spirit."

C. Baptism.
John the Baptist was baptizing in water. The people all knew that because John said, ""I baptize with water those who repent of their sins and turn to God. But someone is coming soon who is far greater than I am—so much greater that I am not even worthy even to be His slave and carry His sandals. He will baptize you with the Holy Spirit and with fire." (Matt 3:11, NLT). There is your water and Spirit connection.

> Titus 3:5 adds, "He saved us, not on the basis of deeds which we have done in righteousness, but according to His mercy, by the washing of regeneration and renewing by the Holy Spirit," (Tit 3:5, NASB95).

Clearly, the washing of regeneration refers to baptism. Regeneration associates with new birth and, "hence renovation, the production of a new life." Strong's Greek Number 3824.

2. Forgiveness of sin is associated with baptism:

The Bible says to be baptized "for the forgiveness of your sins." (Acts 2:38, NASB95). It does not say that baptism is "to show your sins have been forgiven." Baptism is not "because your sins have been forgiven," but "for forgiveness."

> Acts 22:16 says, "And now, why delay? What are you waiting for? Get up and be baptized., and have your sins washed away by, calling on the name of the Lord." (Acts 15-17, NLT). Paul had become a believer, had repented on the road to Damascus three days earlier (Acts 9:9), but his sins had not been forgiven!

3. Salvation is associated with baptism:

> Jesus saId, "Anyone who believes and is baptized will be saved. But anyone who refuses to believe will be condemned." (Mark 16:16, NLT). The last phrase is not an argument against baptism since it is irrelevant whether a person is baptized or not if they don't believe. They are still condemned.

> 1 Peter 3:21 says, "And corresponding to that, [i.e., the eight brought to safety through water via the ark] baptism now saves you - not the removal of dirt from

> the flesh, but an appeal to God for a good conscience – through the resurrection of Jesus Christ," (1 Pet. 3:21, NASB95).

> Paul said, "For I am not ashamed of the gospel, for it is the power of God for salvation to everyone who believes, to the Jew first and also to the Greek." (Rom.ans 1:16, NASB95).

The Gospel consists of His death, burial and resurrection.

> "Now I make known to you, brethren, the gospel which I preached to you, which also you received, in which also you stand, by which also you are saved, if you hold fast the word which I preached to you, unless you believed in vain. For I delivered to you as of first importance what I also received, that Christ died for our sins according to the Scriptures, and that He was buried, and that He was raised on the third day according to the Scriptures, and that He appeared to Cephas, then to the twelve." (1 Cor. 15:1-5, NASB95).

We identify with, and re-enact, that death, burial, and resurrection in baptism — dead to sin, buried with Christ, and risen to new life.

4. Being in Christ is associated with baptism:

> Romans 6:3 says, "Or do you not know that all of us who have been baptized into Christ Jesus have been baptized into His death?" (Rom. 6:3, NASB95). That this refers to water baptism is clear from the words, "Therefore we have been buried with Him through baptism into death, in order that as Christ was raised from the dead through the glory of the Father, so we too might walk in newness of life." (Rom. 6:4, NASB95).

> Galatians 3:27 says, "For all of you who were baptized into Christ have clothed yourselves with Christ." NASB95). To be clothed with is to be "in Christ." It is "to sink into" Christ. Strong's Greek Number 1746.

If any one believes they can be saved outside of Christ, they are deceived. Surely that tenet is manifest.

But what about infants?

We do not baptize infants because there are two Biblical antecedents to baptism an infant cannot fulfill. Those antecedents are:

1. **Belief:** Those who believe may be baptized according to: Acts 2:36-38 and Acts 8:37. Belief is implied necessary when Paul told the Ethiopian eunuch he could be baptized if he believed.

2. **Repentance:** Those who repent of sin may be baptized.;: Acts 2:38 makes that clear.

A valid question to ponder is: "Why people are not baptized?" I can conceive of only three "reasons," which are not indeed valid reasons at all:

1. **Ignorance.** They just don't know about baptism. Nobody has told them, so they don't understand. With so many opportunities to know, ignorance is no excuse

2. **Lack of opportunity.** After believing in Jes, there is no opportunityfor a person to be immersed. They believe the witness of the passenger next to them in the airplane, but it crashes before you they can land and go to church. Consider instead of these extraordinary situations: what about the numberless opportunities they already passed up?

3. **Rebellion.** They know, but for whatever reason, they stubbornly refuse to submit. But to rebellion, God says, "I am Lord." There is no salvation for those who do not obey God's commands.

It is conceivable that God might take the first two into consideration, but He will never overlook or condone the third! That is an absolute, willful rejection of Christ as Lord. No one can rightfully make a claim to salvation to whom Jesus is not Lord!

So, let's cut the "Gospel lite" and go for the "Gospel Light" without condition or equivocation. Not only is our integrity at stake, but so are the peoples' souls.

Do Bible things in the Bible way and be blessed.

ETERNAL SECURITY

Some people hold to an unbiblical doctrine, variously stated as, "Eternal Security," "Once in Grace, Always in Grace," "Once Saved, Always Saved," and "The Perseverance of the Saints."

They mean by that doctrine, that if a person is truly saved, they can never lose salvation. That would be comforting if it were true. But we don't get the luxury of going by what would be comforting if it is not true. The Bible teaches that it is possible to lose salvation.

If we deny Unconditional Eternal Security, that leads to significant questions:

1. **Is salvation conditional?** That is, are there any "if's" about it?

2. **Is free-will eliminated once saved?** We chose Christ as Lord, but can't we change our mind?

Anwer to Question 1: If there are passages with the conditional "if" attached, salvation is conditioned upon that factor. Consider some examples

> "I am the true vine, and My Father is the vinedresser. Every branch in Me that does not bear fruit, He takes away; and every *branch* that bears fruit, He prunes it so that it may bear more fruit. You are already clean because of the word which I have spoken to you. Abide in Me, and I in you. As the branch cannot bear fruit of itself unless it abides in the vine, so neither *can* you unless you abide in Me. I am the vine, you are the branches; he who abides in Me and I in him, he bears much fruit, for apart from Me you can do nothing. **IF** anyone does not abide in Me, he is thrown away as a branch and dries up; and they gather them, and cast them into the fire and they are burned. **IF** you abide in Me, and My words abide in you, ask whatever you wish, and it will be done for you. My Father is glorified by this, that you bear much fruit, and so prove to be My disciples. Just as the Father has loved Me, I have also loved you; abide in My love. **IF** you keep My commandments, you will abide in My love; just as I have kept My Father's commandments and abide in His

love." (John 15:1-10, NASB95; italics in original, bold emphasis added).

"But **IF** some of the branches were broken off, and you, being a wild olive, were grafted in among them and became partaker with them of the rich root of the olive tree, do not be arrogant toward the branches; but **IF** you are arrogant, *remember that* it is not you who *supports* the root, but the root supports you. You will say then, 'Branches were broken off so that I might be grafted in.' Quite right, they were broken off for their unbelief, but you stand by your faith. Do not be conceited, but fear; for **IF** God did not spare the natural branches, He will not spare you, either. Behold then the kindness and severity of God; to those who fell, severity, but to you, God's kindness, **IF** you continue in His kindness; otherwise you also will be cut off." (Rom.ans 11:17-22, NASB95; italics in original, bold emphasis added).

"Now I make known to you, brethren, the gospel which I preached to you, which also you received, in which also you stand, by which also you are saved, **IF** you hold fast the word which I preached to you, unless you believed in vain." (1 Cor. 15:1-2, NASB95; bold emphasis added).

"And although you were formerly alienated and hostile in mind, *engaged* in evil deeds, yet He has now reconciled you in His fleshly body through death, in order to present you before Him holy and blameless and beyond reproach — **IF** indeed you continue in the faith firmly established and steadfast, and not moved away from the hope of the gospel that you have heard, which was proclaimed in all creation under heaven, and of which I, Paul, was made a minister." (Col. 1:21-23, NASB95; italics in original, bold emphasis added).

If these "ifs" don't mean "conditional upon," then what do they mean?

Answer to Question two: Can the Christian cast off faith and quit believing?

Paul wrote to some who had done that, saying,

> Behold I, Paul, say to you that if you receive circumcision, Christ will be of no benefit to you. And I testify again to every man who receives circumcision, that he is under obligation to keep the whole Law. You

> have been severed from Christ, you who are seeking to be justified by law; you have fallen from grace. (Gal. 5:2-4, NASB95).

Note that l refer to trying to be saved by means other than Jesus alone—in the case of the Galatians, they preferred Law. But Paul said that this severed them from Christ and caused their fall from grace.

If so, then:

1. Either salvation can be forfeit since grace is one of the two essential bases for salvation, or

2. we must conclude that one can be saved without grace.

But go to the Word:

> But what does it say? "The word is near you, in your mouth and in your heart"—that is, *the word of faith which we are preaching*, that if you confess with your mouth Jesus as Lord, and believe in your heart that God raised Him from the dead, you will be saved; for with the heart a person believes, resulting in righteousness, and with the mouth he confesses, resulting in salvation. (Rom. 10:8-10, NASB95, italics in original).

Remember Paul spoke in Romans 6 to those believers who, by faith, were baptized.

> And without faith it is impossible to please *Him*, for he who comes to God must believe that He is and *that* He is a rewarder of those who seek Him. (Heb. 11:6, NASB95).

Passages indicating the possibility of casting off faith:

> Take care, brethren, that there not be in any one of you an evil, unbelieving heart that falls away from the living God. But encourage one another day after day, as long as it is *still* called "Today," so that none of you will be hardened by the deceitfulness of sin. For we have become partakers of Christ, if we hold fast the beginning of our assurance firm until the end, while it is said, "Today if you hear His voice, Do not harden your hearts, as when they provoked Me." For who provoked *Him* when they had heard? Indeed, did not all those who came out of Egypt *led* by Moses? And with whom was He angry for forty years? Was it not with those who sinned, whose bodies fell in the wilderness? And to whom did He swear that they would not enter His rest, but to those who were disobedient? So we see that they

were not able to enter because of unbelief. (Heb. 3:12-19, NASB95; italics in original).

It is a trustworthy statement:

For if we died with Him, we will also live with Him

If we endure, we will also reign with Him;

If we deny Him, He also will deny us;

If we are faithless, He remains faithful, for He cannot deny Himself." (2 Tim. 2:11-13, NASB95).

If it is possible to cast off faith, then we are not believers, if we are not believers, then we are not saved!

Can a Christian be cut off from Christ?

Galatians 5:4 indicates that one can be:

You have been severed from Christ, you who are seeking to be justified by law; you have fallen from grace. (Gal. 5:4, NASB95).

Being united to Christ is essential to salvation.

You cannot be severed from that to which you were never connected.

If one can be severed from Christ:

1. Either they are still saved without Him, or

2. they cease to be saved.

Can a Christian fall from grace?

Grace is the other element in salvation and it is not an inward work of some sort. Grace is God's unmerited favor.

There are scriptures showing that one can fall. For example:

> "You have been severed from Christ, you who are seeking to be justified by law; you have fallen from grace." (Gal. 5:4, NASB95).

If one can fall from grace:

1. Either they are still saved without grace or

2. they are lost having fallen from grace.

Can a Christian experience new life and then turn from God? The Bible says:

> For if, after they have escaped the defilements of the world by the knowledge of the Lord and Savior Jesus Christ, they are again entangled in them and are overcome, the last state has become worse for them than the first. For it would be better for them not to have known the way of righteousness, than having known it, to turn away from the holy commandment handed on to them. It has happened to them according to the true proverb, "A dog returns to its own vomit," and, "A sow, after washing, *returns* to wallowing in the mire." (2 Pet. 2:20-22, NASB95; italics in original).

Hebrews 6:4-10also indicates that they can:

> For in the case of those who have once been enlightened and have tasted of the heavenly gift and have been made partakers of the Holy Spirit, and have tasted the good word of God and the powers of the age to come, and *then* have fallen away, it is impossible to renew them again to repentance, since they again crucify to themselves the Son of God and put Him to open shame. For ground that drinks the rain which often falls on it and brings forth vegetation useful to those for whose sake it is also tilled, receives a blessing from God; but if it yields thorns

> and thistles, it is worthless and close to being cursed, and it ends up being burned. But, beloved, we are convinced of better things concerning you, and things that accompany salvation, though we are speaking in this way. For God is not unjust so as to forget your work and the love which you have shown toward His name, in having ministered and in still ministering to the saints. (Heb. 6:4-10, NASB95; italics in original).

Some might argue, "But they only 'tasted' they didn't really experience life. They just came close to it."

But Hebrews 2:9 shows that Jesus "tasted" death—did He die, or just come close to it?

If one can fall away, or turn from God, then

1. Either they are still saved without God or

2. they are not saved any longer.

Does sin bring death to Christians as it does to non-Christians?

To say not, means that all sins, past, present, and future are already forgiven and have no need of confession.

The Bible assures us that sin does bring death:

> So then, brethren, we are under obligation, not to the flesh, to live according to the flesh—for if you are living according to the flesh, you must die; but if by the Spirit you are putting to death the deeds of the body, you will live." (Rom. 8:12-13, NASB95).

> Blessed is a man who perseveres under trial; for once he has been approved, he will receive the crown of life which *the Lord* has promised to those who love Him. Let no one say when he is tempted, "I am being tempted by God"; for God cannot be tempted by evil, and He Himself does not tempt anyone. But each one is tempted when he is carried away and enticed by his own lust. Then when lust has conceived, it gives birth to sin; and when sin is accomplished, it brings forth death. Do not be deceived, my beloved brethren." (Jas. 1:12-16, NASB95; italics in original).

Further,

> My brethren, if any among you strays from the truth and one turns him back, let him know that he who turns a sinner from the error of his way will save his soul from death and will cover a multitude of sins. (Jas. 5:19-20, NASB95).

...seeing that His divine power has granted to us everything pertaining to life and godliness, through the true knowledge of Him who called us by His own glory and excellence. For by these He has granted to us His precious and magnificent promises, so that by them you may become partakers of *the* divine nature, having escaped the corruption that is in the world by lust. Now for this very reason also, applying all diligence, in your faith supply moral excellence, and in *your* moral excellence, knowledge, and in *your* knowledge, self-control, and in *your* self-control, perseverance, and in *your* perseverance, godliness, and in *your* godliness, brotherly kindness, and in *your* brotherly kindness, love. For if these *qualities* are yours and are increasing, they render you neither useless nor unfruitful in the true knowledge of our Lord Jesus Christ. For he who lacks these *qualities* is blind or shortsighted, having forgotten *his* purification from his former sins. Therefore, brethren, be all the more diligent to make certain about His calling and choosing you; for as long as you practice these things, you will never stumble; for in this way the entrance into the eternal kingdom of our Lord and Savior Jesus Christ will be abundantly supplied to you." (2 Peter 1:3-11, NASB; italics in original).

If death is not condemnation, what is it?

There are two extremes to avoid at all costs: The first is to believe that we can never, under any circumstances, forfeit salvation. That leads to all sorts of immorality and laxness in Christian living.

The second is to imagine that we forfeit salvation every time we sin. That leads to all sorts of fear and angst.

The truth is, when we sin (and we do), God immediately seeks to restore us. The Holy Spirit convicts us of sin. God may send a Christian brother to admonish us. Consequences of our sin may cause us to repent. There are many ways in which God says, "Turn again and be forgiven." We then have a choice: to heed or to rebel. To heed is to repent and find forgiveness in the Lord. To rebel is to go on willfully sinning and rejecting Christ as Lord - and forfeiting salvation.

> Dear friends, if we deliberately continue sinning after we have received a full knowledge of the truth, there is no other sacrifice that will cover these sins. There will be nothing to look forward to but the terrible expectation of God's judgment and the raging fire that will consume his enemies. Anyone who refused to obey the law of

> Moses was put to death without mercy on the testimony of two or three witnesses. Think how much more terrible the punishment will be for those who have trampled on the Son of God and have treated the blood of the covenant as if it were common and unholy. Such people have insulted and enraged the Holy Spirit who brings God's mercy to his people. (Heb. 10:26-29, NLT).

That was said, not to cause us to doubt our salvation, but to ensure it! Remain faithful. Abide in Jesus. And then, and only then, are you eternally secure.

THE "SINNER'S PRAYER" INVITING JESUS INTO YOUR HEART "JUST RAISE YOUR HAND"

I want to address the human idea of "Inviting Jesus into your heart," "praying the sinner's prayer" or "To accept Christ, just raise your hand." While those things are not bad in themselves, they are things some *man* made up and are not ever commanded by God or taught anywhere in Scripture. I challenge anyone, anywhere, at any time to show one single verse of the Bible that says, "invite Jesus into your heart," or that commands us to "pray the sinner's prayer," or to "just raise your hand."

We do see the Publican in Luke beating his chest in sorrow, saying, "O God, be merciful to me, for I am a sinner." (Luke 18:13, NLT). And, we do see Jesus saying to him, "I tell you, this sinner, not the Pharisee, returned home justified before God. For the proud will be humbled, but the humble will be honored." (Luke 18:14, (NLT).

But where is the command for anyone to pray that prayer? Where is there any indication of "oughtness" to that text? Where are we told to do that? Where is the teaching that this is to be a universal and sufficient practice?

Wasn't the tax collector justified by that prayer?

Yes, but he is not a model of Christian conversion. He lived under the Old Testament Law and the old covenant (which was replaced by the New Covenant, instituted only when Christ died! The old was made obsolete by the new!).

Nothing wrong with reciting a prayer asking for salvation, but it is not taught or commanded in the New Testament.

It is an inadequate and unauthorized addition to, or more truly, substitution for, what is commanded.

THE RAPTURE

Some believe in a rapture of believers, where Christians around the world will be taken up into heaven prior to the unleashing of the cataclysmic events that most associate with the end- times. Images of empty piles of clothes and cars whose drivers had suddenly disappeared have been a part of the popular understanding of The Rapture for decades, and many do not question whether such an event plays out like this in the Bible. But how did we get here? Where did these popular understandings of the rapture come from, and how do they compare to what the church historically taught regarding the rapture and Final Judgement?

The doctrines of "The Rapture" and other end- times issues have confused, and even divided, the church. One's interpretation of these events has, in many congregations, become a test of fellowship as many follow the script: "If you don't believe as I believe, we cannot have fellowship."

I want, in this article, to consider the rapture of believers, especially the chronological order of being "taken" or "left" and the meaning of those words.

First, what we must understand is what is meant by the word "rapture" and from where does the idea originate? The word comes from the Latin word, "rapiemur," which means "caught up." The word is never used in any ancient text but comes from the Vulgate, a Latin translation by Jerome, a Catholic priest. It is found in 1 Thessalonians 4:16-17:

> For the Lord Himself will descend from heaven with a shout, with the voice of the archangel and with the trumpet of God, and the dead in Christ will rise first. Then we who are alive and remain will be caught up together with them in the clouds to meet the Lord in the air, and so we shall always be with the Lord. (1 Thess. 4:16-17, NASB95).

Now, here's where the disagreement begins. In what order are the saved and lost "taken" or "left," respectively?

Before hearing my opinion on that, listen to Jesus:

> But of that day and hour no one knows, not even the angels of heaven, nor the Son, but the Father alone. For the coming of the Son of Man will be just like the days of Noah. For as in those days before the flood they were eating and drinking, marrying and giving in marriage, until the day that Noah entered the ark, and they did not understand until the flood came and took them

all away; so will the coming of the Son of Man be. Then there will be two men in the field; one will be taken and one will be left. Two women will be grinding at the mill; one will be taken and one will be left. (Matt. 24:36-41, NASB95).

Consider, too, Jesus' parables:

Jesus presented another parable to them,

The kingdom of heaven may be compared to a man who sowed good seed in his field. But while his men were sleeping, his enemy came and sowed tares among the wheat, and went away. But when the wheat sprouted and bore grain, then the tares became evident also. The slaves of the landowner came and said to him, "Sir, did you not sow good seed in your field? How then does it have tares?" And he said to them, "An enemy has done this!" The slaves said to him, "Do you want us, then, to go and gather them up?" But he said, "No; for while you are gathering up the tares, you may uproot the wheat with them. Allow both to grow together until the harvest; and in the time of the harvest I will say to the reapers, 'First gather up the tares and bind them in bundles to burn them up; but gather the wheat into my barn.'" (Matt. 13:24-30, NASB95).

His disciples came to Him and said,

> "Explain to us the parable of the tares of the field." And He said, "The one who sows the good seed is the Son of Man, and the field is the world; and as for the good seed, these are the sons of the kingdom; and the tares are the sons of the evil one; and the enemy who sowed them is the devil, and the harvest is the end of the age; and the reapers are angels. So just as the tares are gathered up and burned with fire, so shall it be at the end of the age. The Son of Man will send forth His angels, and they will gather out of His kingdom all stumbling blocks, and those who commit lawlessness, and will throw them into the furnace of fire; in that place there will be weeping and gnashing of teeth. Then THE RIGHTEOUS WILL SHINE FORTH AS THE SUN in the kingdom of their Father. He who has ears, let him hear." (Matt. 13:36-43, NASB95)

> Again, the kingdom of heaven is like a dragnet cast into the sea, and gathering *fish* of every kind; and when it was filled, they drew it up on the beach; and they sat down

and gathered the good *fish* into containers, but the bad they threw away. So it will be at the end of the age; the angels will come forth and take out the wicked from among the righteous, and will throw them into the furnace of fire; in that place there will be weeping and gnashing of teeth. (Matt. 13:47-50, NASB95; italics in original).

Now reason with me because we already have a Scriptural precedent for this event:

Jesus said His coming would be as in Noah's day. Apparently, Noah had one hundred and twenty years to lead his neighbors to repentance, but they would have no part of it. So, God sent the flood, and everyone drowned.

A. Who was taken away?

B. who was left?

Is it not clear? The wicked were taken and Noah, his wife, their three sons, and their wives were the only people left.

Jesus said that:

1. a. His angels would take the weeds first and the good crop would be left and gathered up.

2. b. His angels would take the bad fish first and discard them and then they would gather the good fish that were left.

Is it not clear? The bad were removed (taken) first and then the good were left.

In my opinion, the "Rapturist" doctrine has it backward in believing that the righteous will be taken for 1,000 years, while the unsaved will be left behind on Earth.

If you were to hear or read these scriptures without any preconceived notions, and pay attention to the order Jesus established, would you believe that the saved are taken and the unsaved left? I don't think so. How could we see any order other than what Jesus taught?

Forget what any church father, theologian, or scholar has to say and heed Jesus Himself.

The problem with Rapture Theology is that the order of dealing with the lost and saved is backward.

There is yet another Unbiblical misconception.

GOD WON'T GIVE US MORE THAN WE CAN HANDLE

Of course, He gives us more than we can handle… – on our own.

Examples:

Noah, of whom we read:,

> Now the earth was corrupt in the sight of God, and the earth was filled with violence. God looked on the earth, and behold, it was corrupt; for all flesh had corrupted their way upon the earth. Then God said to Noah, "The end of all flesh has come before Me; for the earth is filled with violence because of them; and behold, I am about to destroy them with the earth. Make for yourself an ark of gopher wood; you shall make the ark with rooms, and shall cover it inside and out with pitch. This is how you shall make it: the length of the

> ark three hundred cubits, its breadth fifty cubits, and its height thirty cubits. You shall make a window for the ark, and finish it to a cubit from the top; and set the door of the ark in the side of it; you shall make it with lower, second, and third decks. Behold, I, even I am bringing the flood of water upon the earth, to destroy all flesh in which is the breath of life, from under heaven; everything that is on the earth shall perish." (Gen. 6:11-17, NASB95).

Noah had no idea of what an ark was. He had no concept of a flood.

So. God gave him the task of building something of which he knew nothing to be saved from a danger about which he was totally ignorant!

That's a complete overload for Noah– unless Noah had His help!

Moses felt completely overburdened. Check it out:

> The rabble who were among them had greedy desires; and also the sons of Israel wept again and said, "Who will give us meat to eat? We remember the fish which we used to eat free in Egypt, the cucumbers and the melons and the leeks and the onions

and the garlic, but now our appetite is gone. There is nothing at all to look at except this manna."

Now the manna was like coriander seed, and its appearance like that of bdellium. The people would go about and gather *it* and grind *it* between two millstones or beat *it* in the mortar, and boil *it* in the pot and make cakes with it; and its taste was as the taste of cakes baked with oil. When the dew fell on the camp at night, the manna would fall with it.

Now Moses heard the people weeping throughout their families, each man at the doorway of his tent; and the anger of the LORD was kindled greatly, and Moses was displeased. So Moses said to the LORD, "Why have You been so hard on Your servant? And why have I not found favor in Your sight, that You have laid the burden of all this people on me? Was it I who conceived all this people? Was it I who brought them forth, that You should say to me, 'Carry them in your bosom as a nurse carries a nursing infant, to the land which You swore to their fathers? Where am I to get meat to give to all this people? For they weep before me, saying, 'Give us meat that we may eat!'

> I alone am not able to carry all this people, because it is too burdensome for me. So if You are going to deal thus with me, please kill me at once, if I have found favor in Your sight, and do not let me see my wretchedness." (Num. 11:4-15, NASB95, emphasis in original).

Gideon was given an undoable task — undoable by him alone.

> Then the angel of the LORD came and sat under the oak that was in Ophrah, which belonged to Joash the Abiezrite as his son Gideon was beating out wheat in the wine press in order to save *it* from the Midianites. The angel of the LORD appeared to him and said to him, "The LORD is with you, O valiant warrior." Then Gideon said to him, "O my lord, if the LORD is with us, why then has all this happened to us? And where are all His miracles which our fathers told us about, saying, 'Did not the LORD bring us up from Egypt?' But now the LORD has abandoned us and given us into the hand of Midian." The LORD looked at him and said, "Go in this your strength and deliver Israel from the hand of Midian. Have I not sent you?" He said to Him, "O Lord, how shall I deliver Israel? Behold, my family is

the least in Manasseh, and I am the youngest in my father's house." But the LORD said to him, "Surely I will be with you, and you shall defeat Midian as one man." (Judg. 6:11-16, NASB95; emphasis in original).

Gideon was told to tear down the local altar to Ashera and to use its wood to make an offering to offer a sacrifice to God.

But why? For what reason would Gods over-encumber us?

1. To make us realize our limitations.

David prayed, "Have compassion on me, LORD, for I am weak. Heal me, LORD, for my bones are in agony." (Ps. 6:2, NLT; emphasis in original).

2. To make us rely on Him, not the self.

Paul wrote, "In fact, we expected to die. But as a result, we stopped relying on ourselves and learned to rely only on God, who raises the dead." (2 Cor. 1:9, (NLT2).

3. To cleanse us of pride.

Paul wrote, "Because of the surpassing greatness of the revelations, for this reason, to keep me from exalting myself, there was given me a thorn in the flesh, a messenger of Satan to torment me—to keep me from exalting myself!

Concerning this I implored the Lord three times that it might leave me. And He has said to me, 'My grace is sufficient for you, for power is perfected in weakness.' Most gladly, therefore, I will rather boast about my weaknesses, so that the power of Christ may dwell in me. Therefore I am well content with weaknesses, with insults, with distresses, with persecutions, with difficulties, for Christ's sake; for when I am weak, then I am strong." (2 Cor. 12:7-10, NASB95).

4. To strengthen and develop us.

Paul wrote after being persecuted:

> At my first defense no one supported me, but all deserted me; may it not be counted against them. But the Lord stood with me and strengthened me, so that through me the proclamation might be fully accomplished, and that all the Gentiles might hear; and I was rescued out of the lion's mouth. (2 Tim. 4:16-17, NASB95).

5. To demonstrate His power to others.

Shadrach, Meshach and Abednego refused to worship King Nebuchadnezzar's Golden Idol. They were cast into a fiery furnace, and survived. Not because they were wearing asbestos undies, but because they were committed and served the Lord whole heartedly! Nebuchadnezzar exclaimed,

"Therefore I make a decree that any people, nation or tongue that speaks anything offensive against the God of Shadrach, Meshach and Abednego shall be torn limb from limb and their houses reduced to a rubbish heap, inasmuch as there is no other god who is able to deliver in this way." Then the king caused Shadrach, Meshach and Abednego to prosper in the province of Babylon. (Dan. 3:29-30, NASB95).

OTHER ISSUES

I am amazed at the gullibility of God's people. If a book becomes a bestseller, people buy it and blindly believe it must be true.

As an example, where in the Bible are we commanded to pray the "Prayer of Jabez" or are promised an answer to it? Why didn't Jesus teach His disciples that prayer instead of the one we call the Lord's prayer?

Where in the Bible are we promised that if we draw a circle around something and pray for it, we will obtain it? That's not Scripture, that's based on a dubious legend.

And what about all these accounts of visiting heaven and coming back with a report of what was seen? Did not the Apostle Paul declare,

> "Boasting is necessary, though it is not profitable; but I will go on to visions and revelations of the Lord. I know a man in Christ who fourteen years ago—whether in the body I do not know, or out of the body I

> do not know, God knows—such a man was caught up to the third heaven. And I know how such a man—whether in the body or apart from the body I do not know, God knows— was caught up into Paradise and heard inexpressible words, which a man is not permitted to speak." (2 Cor. 12:1-4, NASB95).

How then dare anyone to presume to speak those "inexpressible words"?

I merely point out all these issues so that we have the right answer to the question, "But, is that in the Bible?"

Until we find the answer to that question and live by it, we will be continually misled down the trail of human tradition and false doctrine.

I urge you to be one of those fore-runners who care more for what God's Word has said than what the tradition and wisdom of man propounds.